Jefferson-Madison Regional Library

GIFT OF
EDNA H. MUSSER

AARON RODGERS

BY PAUL HOBLIN

Jefferson Madison
Regional Library
Charlottesville, Virginia

Published by ABDO Publishing Company, PO Box 398166, Minneapolis, MN 55439. Copyright © 2012 by Abdo Consulting Group, Inc. International copyrights reserved in all countries. No part of this book may be reproduced in any form without written permission from the publisher. SportsZone™ is a trademark and logo of ABDO Publishing Company.

Printed in the United States of America,
North Mankato, Minnesota
092011
012012

THIS BOOK CONTAINS AT LEAST 10% RECYCLED MATERIALS.

Editor: Chrös McDougall
Copy Editor: Anna Comstock
Series Design: Craig Hinton
Cover and Interior Production: Kazuko Collins

Photo Credits: David Stluka/AP Images, cover, 1, 4, 7, 27; Morry Gash/AP Images, 9, 19; Paul Sakuma/AP Images, 10, 15; David Zalubowski/AP Images, 13; Julie Jacobson/AP Images, 16; Tony Gutierrez/AP Images, 21; Mike Roemer/AP Images, 22; Greg Trott/AP Images, 25; Kevin Terrell/AP Images, 29

Library of Congress Cataloging-in-Publication Data

Hoblin, Paul.
 Aaron Rodgers : Super Bowl MVP / by Paul Hoblin.
    p. cm. — (Playmakers)
 Includes index.
 ISBN 978-1-61783-295-6
 1. Rodgers, Aaron, 1983- 2. Football players—United States—Biography—Juvenile literature. 3. Quarterbacks (Football—United States—Biography—Juvenile literature. 4. Green Bay Packers (Football team—Juvenile literature. 5. Super Bowl (45th : 2011 : Arlington, Tex—Juvenile literature. I. Title.
 GV939.R6235H63 2012
 796.332092—dc23
 [B]
                                                    2011039551

TABLE OF CONTENTS

CHAPTER 1
Championship Childhood.................................... 5

CHAPTER 2
Is Anybody Out There?... 11

CHAPTER 3
Dropping in the Draft 17

CHAPTER 4
Booing and (Super) Bowling 23

Fun Facts and Quotes... 30

Web Links... 30

Glossary 31

Further Resources and Index 32

Aaron Rodgers

CHAPTER 1

CHAMPIONSHIP CHILDHOOD

The fans at Lambeau Field in Wisconsin love when their Green Bay Packers score a touchdown. The players sometimes celebrate scoring by doing the Lambeau Leap. That is when they jump into the arms of the fans sitting in the front row.

Aaron Rodgers is the Packers' quarterback. And he has his own way of celebrating. Growing up, Aaron and his two brothers loved watching professional

> **Aaron Rodgers has made many great plays for the Green Bay Packers.**

wrestling. The best wrestlers got to wear giant gold belts. That meant they were titleholders. So after a good play, Aaron pretends to strap on an imaginary belt just like the wrestlers.

Aaron also loved other sports growing up. He was a great all-around athlete. Two of his best sports were baseball and basketball. But football was Aaron's favorite sport.

Aaron was already watching National Football League (NFL) games by age two. He grew up in Chico, California. So he always cheered for the San Francisco 49ers. Aaron showed football skills early, too. He could throw a football through a tire hung from a tree by the time he was five. He could also toss a football over the roof of a house.

Aaron's father, Ed, had also been a football player. He played on a semiprofessional team. After Ed stopped playing,

> Aaron's older brother is Luke. Aaron and Luke play catch together in the off-season. Sometimes they play on a hill. One brother stands at the bottom, and the other brother stands at the top. Aaron's younger brother is Jordan. He became a backup quarterback for Vanderbilt University in Tennessee in 2010.

Aaron poses with his family after he led the Packers to victory in Super Bowl XLV.

he decided to become a chiropractor. So the family had to move to Oregon for three years so Ed could go to school.

Moving was not Aaron's biggest concern at the time, though. The 49ers traded Joe Montana that year. Montana had been the 49ers' star quarterback for years. And he was Aaron's favorite player. Aaron wanted to win a Super Bowl someday, just like Montana. But now he felt as if he had lost his hero.

Few people believed Aaron would be like Montana. They did not think Aaron would ever be good enough to play in the NFL. He was talented. But he was also small. In fact, his parents did not let him play organized football for a while when he was young. They worried he would get hurt. Aaron was still barely over five feet tall when he entered high school. Most NFL quarterbacks are taller than six feet.

But Aaron did not give up. He also did not stop growing. He was nearly six feet tall by his junior year. Aaron was also becoming a star. His family had since returned to Chico. Aaron was Pleasant Valley High School's best player. He threw for 2,303 yards as a senior. That was a school record. He even threw six touchdown passes in one game. Aaron was a star student, too. He earned good grades and did really well on tests.

People in Chico knew that Aaron was talented. But few people outside the city seemed to notice. Maybe it was because

> Aaron can throw a football very well. He also has some talent at throwing a baseball. Aaron was a pitcher on his high school baseball team. He threw the ball more than 90 miles per hour.

Few people believed Aaron (12) would ever be doing the famous Lambeau Leap when he was growing up.

his team had a bad record. Or maybe it was because Aaron was still pretty small. He had grown taller, but he was skinny.

Aaron felt invisible. Not one college team offered him a scholarship. The only coach who wanted Aaron was Craig Rigsbee. He was a junior college coach at Butte College. He lived only a block from Aaron. After thinking about it for a while, Aaron decided to take him up on the offer.

10 | **Aaron Rodgers**

CHAPTER 2

IS ANYBODY OUT THERE?

Aaron Rodgers decided to go to a junior college for one big reason: he wanted to play football. But for a while, it looked like he might not get to do that. Butte College already had a quarterback named Bryan Botts. He had been playing for the team for two years. Botts wanted to be the starter as much as Rodgers did. Coach Craig Rigsbee asked his assistant coaches who they thought should start. All of them picked Botts.

Rodgers had to prove himself in junior college before earning a scholarship to the University of California.

Only Coach Rigsbee believed Rodgers should be the starting quarterback. He thought Rodgers was too talented to sit on the bench. The freshman quarterback showed off that talent during an early-season practice. Rodgers moved to his right. Then he threw a fifty-yard pass to the other corner of the field. Not very many quarterbacks can do that. Rigsbee was impressed. Rodgers was named Butte's starting quarterback before the first game.

It did not take long for Rodgers to show that Rigsbee had made the right choice. The quarterback quickly became a star. He led his team to a 10–1 record. He also threw 28 touchdowns. By the end of the year, Butte was ranked second in the nation among junior colleges.

Those close to Rodgers's team could see his skills. He hoped others would see them as well. Many junior college

> Coach Jeff Tedford is known for his ability to coach quarterbacks. Trent Dilfer, David Carr, and Akili Smith are just three of the many college quarterbacks who became NFL starters after working with Tedford. Of all these quarterbacks, Rodgers is considered the best.

California coach Jeff Tedford, *left,* **was one of the few people who realized the abilities of Rodgers,** *right.*

players hope to get a scholarship to play at a four-year college. That was Rodgers's goal, too. But no matter how many touchdowns he threw, no one seemed to know he even existed.

The only four-year college coach who did see Rodgers play was Jeff Tedford. He was the coach at the University of California. Tedford came to Butte's practice to see tight end Garrett Cross. Cross was big and fast. He had caught a lot of

> Rodgers left Butte College after only one year. He still loves the school, though. During interviews, he sometimes wears Butte College T-shirts in support of the school that gave him a shot.

passes that year. But Tedford left the practice more excited about the guy throwing Cross the ball. He called Rodgers and offered him a scholarship. Finally, Rodgers had been noticed. He was going to play football at California.

It had taken Rodgers a long time to get a scholarship. But it did not take him long to impress his new team. Rodgers was named Cal's starting quarterback by the fifth game of his first season. Young quarterbacks often make a lot of mistakes. That was not the case with Rodgers. He threw almost 100 passes before throwing an interception. Rodgers finished the year with 19 touchdown passes and only five interceptions. More importantly, Cal went 7–3 in the games that Rodgers started.

Cal was even better the next season. Rodgers started every game. The team went 10–1 during the regular season. That was good enough to win the Pacific-10 Conference. Rodgers's best game was against the University of Southern California.

California fans carry Rodgers after he led the team to a 41–6 win over the rival Stanford Cardinal in 2004.

He completed 23 passes in a row. However, his team ended up losing 23–17.

Despite this loss, Cal had one of its best seasons in years. Rodgers had a great season, too. In just two years, Rodgers had become one of the top college quarterbacks in the nation. Most people thought he was ready for the NFL. Rodgers decided to see if they were right.

Aaron Rodgers

CHAPTER 3

DROPPING IN THE DRAFT

The NFL season ends in February. Excitement about the league continues through April, though. That is when the NFL holds its draft. In the draft, NFL teams take turns selecting college players. Quarterbacks are often very popular. And most people considered Aaron Rodgers to be one of the top two quarterbacks in the 2005 draft.

The San Francisco 49ers had the first pick in that year's draft. They had been Rodgers's favorite

Rodgers holds a Green Bay Packers jersey after the team selected him in the 2005 NFL Draft.

Dropping in the Draft

team growing up. Some people thought the 49ers might select Rodgers. San Francisco indeed selected a quarterback. It was not Rodgers, though. The 49ers instead picked Alex Smith from the University of Utah.

Still, many thought Rodgers was one of the top players available. But he was not the second pick. He was not the third, fourth, or fifth pick either. Before long, Rodgers had lasted through 10 picks, and then 20.

Finally, the Green Bay Packers selected Rodgers with the 24th pick. Rodgers was relieved. It was not necessarily a time for Rodgers to celebrate, though. The Packers already had a star quarterback in Brett Favre. In fact, many believed Favre was one of the best quarterbacks ever. He was also very reliable. Favre had started every game for more than 12 years. It looked unlikely that Rodgers was going to get a chance to play.

> Mike McCarthy was the San Francisco 49ers' offensive coordinator in 2005. He helped make the decision to select Alex Smith over Rodgers. McCarthy later became the Packers' head coach. He has said he feels really lucky to have Rodgers on his team.

Rodgers, *left*, backed up legendary Packers quarterback Brett Favre, *right*, during his first three seasons in the NFL.

Rodgers decided to make the best of the situation. Favre had been very successful. He had even won a Super Bowl. Rodgers knew he could learn a lot from Favre. So, he watched how Favre practiced and prepared for games. Green Bay struggled to win games during Rodgers's rookie year. And he barely played at all during the season. But Rodgers knew that if Favre ever could not play, he would be ready.

It appeared that Rodgers's wait for playing time might be shorter than expected. Favre said he was thinking about retiring after Rodgers's rookie year. But he was back as the Packers' starting quarterback when the season started. Rodgers again barely played that season. Then Favre said he was definitely done playing after Rodgers's second season. However, he again changed his mind.

Rodgers finally got his chance to shine during that third season. Favre was injured in a game against the Dallas Cowboys. The Packers were losing by 17 points when he left the game. But Rodgers filled in and played well for the rest of the game. He brought the Packers to within three points. Green Bay still lost. But people watching the game knew that Rodgers was good enough to be a starting quarterback in the NFL.

Rodgers's opportunity finally came. Favre held a press conference after that season. He announced that his playing

> Rodgers was very thankful when he was told he would finally be Green Bay's starter. He thanked everyone for believing in him. He also promised them that he would not let them down.

Rodgers threw his first touchdown pass during a 2007 game against the Dallas Cowboys.

days were over. He even cried. The Packers announced that Rodgers was now their starting quarterback.

Favre soon changed his mind. But the team was ready to begin a new era with Rodgers. So the Packers traded their legendary quarterback to the New York Jets. That showed Rodgers that the Packers had confidence in him. Win or lose, he was their quarterback of the future.

22 Aaron Rodgers

CHAPTER 4

BOOING AND (SUPER) BOWLING

Aaron Rodgers's teammates and coaches were confident that he was going to be a good quarterback. But not all Packers fans agreed. Brett Favre had been the most popular player on the team. He had thrown more career touchdown passes than any other NFL quarterback. More importantly, he had won a Super Bowl.

Many fans questioned the team's decision in trading Favre. They even booed Rodgers at the

> Rodgers made his first NFL start against the rival Minnesota Vikings on September 8, 2008.

beginning of the season. Rodgers did not blame the fans for being angry and sad. He had felt the same way when the San Francisco 49ers traded Joe Montana. Steve Young had replaced Montana as the team's quarterback. He had even led the team to a Super Bowl. But fans still missed Montana.

The situation in Green Bay was similar. Rodgers had one of the best years of any quarterback in the league. He threw for more than 4,000 yards and 28 touchdowns. But his team struggled. And others were still upset about the trade. The Packers had finished 13–3 in Favre's last season. They had even reached the conference title game. Green Bay only won six games in Rodgers's first season as the starter. He also struggled at times late in games.

Rodgers led the Packers to a comeback victory to open the next season. He continued putting up good passing numbers.

> The San Francisco 49ers were still Rodgers's favorite team when he was in college. During games, he wore a Joe Montana T-shirt under his Cal jersey.

Rodgers threw four touchdown passes and ran for one more in his playoff debut, a 51–45 loss to the Arizona Cardinals in 2010.

And most importantly, he started winning. The Packers finished the season 11–5. Then they lost a high-scoring game in the first round of the playoffs. But most NFL experts agreed that Rodgers was now one of the league's best quarterbacks.

Most of the fans who missed Favre had also changed their minds about him before that season. That is because Favre had signed with the Minnesota Vikings. They were one of the

> Rodgers once grew a big mustache. He was sick of Packers fans comparing him to Brett Favre, and he wanted to give them something else to talk about.

Packers' biggest rivals. And Favre and the Vikings beat the Packers twice that season.

Many fans and NFL experts had high expectations for the Packers in 2010. Rodgers had starred in 2009. But people expected him to be even better in 2010. And he was. Rodgers led the Packers to two victories over Favre and the Vikings. But the team suffered some key injuries and struggled a bit. The Packers needed to win their last two games just to make the playoffs. And that is what they did.

The Packers continued playing well in the playoffs. Rodgers threw three touchdowns in their first game. Green Bay beat the Philadelphia Eagles 21–16 on the road. The Packers played even better in the next game. They traveled to Atlanta to play the Falcons. The Falcons had finished with the best record in the conference at 13–3. But Rodgers again threw for three touchdowns and ran for another. Green Bay won 48–21.

Rodgers (12) became a team leader for the Packers soon after taking over as the starting quarterback.

That set up a conference championship showdown against the rival Chicago Bears. Again the Packers were on the road. But this time, Rodgers did not play so well. His teammates made up for it. They led Green Bay to a 21–14 victory. And with that, the Packers were headed to the Super Bowl.

The Packers' opponent was the Pittsburgh Steelers. Many people thought the Steelers were the NFL's best team. After all, their defense gave up the fewest points of any team that season. And Steelers quarterback Ben Roethlisberger had already led the team to two Super Bowl titles. Several experts predicted the Steelers' experience would lead them past the Packers.

They were wrong. It was Rodgers who played like a veteran. He threw two early touchdowns. Meanwhile, Roethlisberger threw two early interceptions. The Packers took a 21–10 lead into halftime. The Steelers did not give up, though. They scored the only touchdown in the third quarter. That led to a wild fourth quarter. Rodgers led the Packers down the field for a touchdown. But the Steelers answered with a touchdown and two-point conversion. Green Bay's lead was cut to three points.

Rodgers led the Packers into field-goal range on the next drive. The Packers' kicker made the field goal and gave his

> Rodgers no longer lives in Chico, California. But the town still loves him. Many teachers and students at Pleasant Valley High School wore green and gold clothing before the Packers' Super Bowl appearance. Some even put on foam yellow caps that looked like pieces of cheese. The Californians dressed like Packers fans!

Packers teammate Clay Matthews holds a title belt as Rodgers holds the Lombardi Trophy as Super Bowl champion in 2011.

team a six-point lead. Now the Packers just needed to stop the Steelers. And they did. The Packers won 31–25. Rodgers was named the Super Bowl's Most Valuable Player. And he was only 27 years old.

As Rodgers held the Super Bowl trophy, someone gave him another award. It was a giant gold belt, just like the ones professional wrestlers wear.

Booing and (Super) Bowling 29

FUN FACTS AND QUOTES

- Aaron Rodgers's mom, Darla, used to sing to Rodgers when he was young. He has loved music ever since. In June 2011, he launched his own record label called Suspended Sunrise Music.

- Rodgers's favorite movie is *The Princess Bride*. He and his childhood friends can quote every line in the movie.

- Rodgers was a really accurate thrower even as a kid. When he played football in front of his neighbor's house, she never worried about him breaking a window. That is because he always threw the ball exactly where he wanted to.

- Rodgers loved football so much as a kid that he brought his own Nerf football to school. His parents told him he was too small to play tackle football. So he looked forward to the touch football games he and his buddies played at recess.

- Rodgers helped organize a charity event called "An Evening with Aaron Rodgers." All the money raised during the event was given to the MACC Fund. The purpose of this fund is to support cancer and blood-disorder research.

WEB LINKS

To learn more about Aaron Rodgers, visit ABDO Publishing Company online at www.abdopublishing.com. Web sites about Rodgers are featured on our Book Links page. These links are routinely monitored and updated to provide the most current information available.

GLOSSARY

accurate
When a quarterback is good at throwing the ball where he wants to.

chiropractor
Someone who is trained to help an injured body heal.

conference
NFL teams are divided into two conferences, and the conference champions meet in the Super Bowl.

draft
A system in which teams in a league select rookies during each off-season.

junior college
A two-year college.

offensive coordinator
The main coach of a football team's offense.

retiring
Ending one's career.

rookie
A first-year player in the NFL.

scholarship
Money awarded to students to help them pay for school. Top athletes earn scholarships to represent a college through its sports teams.

semiprofessional
Something that pays money but not enough to make a living on.

veteran
A player with a lot of experience.

INDEX

Atlanta Falcons, 26

Butte College, 9, 11–13, 14

Chicago Bears, 27

Dallas Cowboys, 20

Favre, Brett, 18–21, 23, 24, 25–26

Green Bay Packers, 5, 18–21, 23–29

Lambeau Field, 5

McCarthy, Mike, 18
Minnesota Vikings, 25–26
Montana, Joe, 7–8, 24

New York Jets, 21
NFL Draft, 17

Pacific–10 Conference, 14
Philadelphia Eagles, 26
Pittsburgh Steelers, 27–29
Pleasant Valley High School, 8–9, 28

Rigsbee, Craig, 9, 11–12
Roethlisberger, Ben, 28

San Francisco 49ers, 6, 7, 17–18, 24
Smith, Alex, 18
Super Bowl, 7, 19, 23, 24, 27–29

Tedford, Jeff, 12, 13–14

University of California, 13, 14–15
University of Southern California, 14–15

Young, Steve, 24

FURTHER RESOURCES

Gulbrandsen, Don. *Green Bay Packers: The Complete Illustrated History*. 3rd ed. Minneapolis: MVP Books, 2011.

Hanrahan, Phil. *Life After Favre: The Green Bay Packers and Their Fans Usher in the Aaron Rodgers Era*. New York: Skyhorse Pub., 2011.

Reischel, Rob. *Green Bay Packers*. Edina, MN: ABDO Publishing Co., 2011.